# READING POWER

Biomes

Oceans

Holly Cefrey

The Rosen Publishing Group's
PowerKids Press™
New York

Published in 2003 by The Rosen Publishing Group, Inc.
29 East 21st Street, New York, NY 10010

Copyright © 2003 by The Rosen Publishing Group, Inc.

All rights reserved. No part of this book may be reproduced in any form without permission in writing from the publisher, except by a reviewer.

First Edition

Book Design: Mindy Liu

Photo Credits: Cover © Karen Huntt Mason/Corbis; pp. 4–5 © Galen Rowell/Corbis; p. 4 (inset) MapArt; p. 7 © David R. Bridge/National Geographic Image Collection; pp. 8–9 © Tony Arruza/Corbis; p. 10 © Bruce Robison/Corbis; p. 11 Mindy Liu; p. 12 © Frank Lane Picture Agency/Corbis; p. 13 (top) © Stuart Westmorland/Corbis; p. 13 (bottom) © Jeffrey L. Rotman/Corbis; pp. 14–15 © Mike Johnson; p. 15 (top) © OSF/P. Parks/Animals Animals; pp. 16–17 © Greg Huglin/SuperStock; pp. 18–19 © Luis Marden/National Geographic Image Collection; p. 18 (inset) © Ralph White/Corbis; p. 20 © Natalie Fobes/Corbis; p. 21 © AFP/Corbis

Library of Congress Cataloging-in-Publication Data

Cefrey, Holly.
  Oceans / Holly Cefrey.
    p. cm. — (Biomes)
  Summary: Describes the fragile ecosystem of oceans.
  Includes bibliographical references (p.   ).
  ISBN 0-8239-6453-1 (lib. bdg.)
  1. Marine ecology—Juvenile literature. 2. Ocean—Juvenile literature. [1. Ocean. 2. Marine ecology. 3. Ecology.] I. Title.
  QH541.5.S3 C34 2003
  577.7—dc21
                                                      2002000178
]

Contents

Ocean Biome 4
Under the Sea 10
Ocean Life 12
The Wind and the Tides 16
Studying the Ocean 18
Glossary 22
Resources 23
Index/Word Count 24
Note 24

Ocean Biome

The ocean biome is the largest biome on the earth. It covers over 70 percent of the earth's surface. The Pacific, Atlantic, Arctic, and Indian Oceans make up the ocean biome.

Most of the water on Earth is found in the oceans. Without the oceans, there would be no life on Earth.

Now You Know

A biome *(BY-ohm)* is a plant and animal community that covers a large part of the earth.

The ocean biome supplies us with food, energy, and minerals. We eat many of the plants and animals living in the ocean. Energy comes from oil and natural gas found in the ocean floor. Minerals, such as sand and gravel, are taken from the bottom of the oceans. These minerals are used to make building materials.

The oceans give us much of the food we eat. These fishermen have caught tuna.

Now You Know

About 97 percent of the earth's water comes from the ocean biome.

The oceans also control weather on Earth. In the summer, the oceans store heat from the sun's warm rays. In the winter, this heat helps warm the earth. The oceans also supply most of our rainwater. As ocean water heats up, it evaporates and rises into the sky as a gas. The gas forms clouds. As the clouds cool, rain or snow falls back to Earth.

Rainwater has no salt in it. This is because the salt in the oceans' water cannot evaporate.

Under the Sea

The ocean floor has deep valleys and large, flat plains. It also has mountain ranges, just like on the surface of the earth. Many of these mountains rise about 5,000 feet above the ocean floor. The ocean floor has underwater volcanoes that erupt, too.

Hatchetfish

Some of the creatures that live in the deep ocean, such as the hatchetfish, are very unusual. Some do not have eyes, and others glow in the dark.

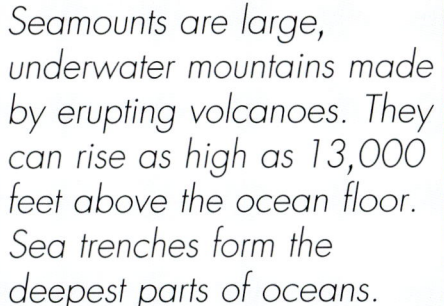
Seamounts are large, underwater mountains made by erupting volcanoes. They can rise as high as 13,000 feet above the ocean floor. Sea trenches form the deepest parts of oceans.

Seamount

Sea trench

Ocean floor

Ocean Life

The three groups of ocean life are the plankton, the nekton, and the benthos. Plankton are plantlike creatures and animals that drift with ocean currents. Nekton are animals that swim freely in the ocean. Fish, squid, and ocean mammals are nekton. Benthos are sea creatures that live on or near the ocean floor.

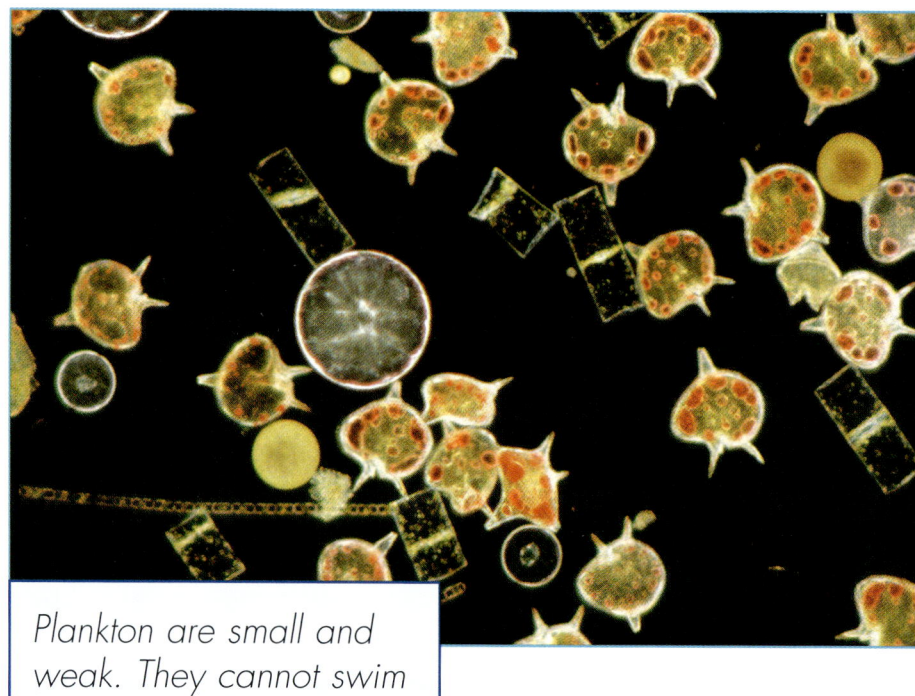

Plankton are small and weak. They cannot swim against ocean currents.

Nekton include ocean mammals, such as these bottlenose dolphins.

Benthos include this false clown fish and the sea anemone in which it is hiding.

Ocean plants and animals grow to many different sizes. Some, such as plankton, are so small they cannot be seen without microscopes. Larger animals, such as the blue whale, can be as long as 100 feet. Plants can live up to 330 feet below the surface of the water. The sunlight that plants need to live does not reach below that point.

Plankton

Blue whale

Blue whales eat many tons of plankton every day.

The Wind and the Tides

The waves in the ocean are mostly caused by wind. Water moves up and down in an ocean wave, not forward. It moves forward when it gets near the shore and crashes on the beach. Tides are the rise and fall of the water's level.

Tsunamis (su-NAH-meehz) are giant ocean waves that are made by earthquakes. They can travel as fast as 600 miles an hour and can be 100 feet high.

Studying the Ocean

Scientists who study the ocean are called oceanographers. Oceanographers use ships up to 300 feet long to explore the ocean. They also have submarines that can bring them deep into the ocean. Studying the ocean helps scientists understand Earth's weather and life in the sea.

In 1977, oceanographers found places in the deep ocean that were home to entire communities of plants and animals. The scientists never knew that these places were there.

This underwater craft can take scientists 1,500 feet under the ocean.

Trash and junk are often dumped into the ocean. This is called pollution. People have polluted the oceans for many years. We need to keep our ocean biome free of pollution so that it continues to provide us with the things we need.

The oil tanker Exxon Valdez *spilled 11 million gallons of oil into the sea when it sank.*

These women are cleaning sea birds that were covered by oil from a spill.

Glossary

currents (**kehr**-uhnts) the flow or stream of water

energy (**ehn**-uhr-jee) power that can be used to produce heat or make machines work

erupt (ih-**ruhpt**) to violently send out steam and lava

evaporate (ih-**vap**-uh-rayt) to change from a liquid into a gas

gravel (**grav**-uhl) small, loose pieces of rock

mammals (**mam**-uhlz) warm-blooded animals with backbones

microscopes (**my**-kruh-skohps) tools that make very small objects look larger

mineral (**mihn**-uhr-uhl) solid matter that comes from the earth

oceanographers (oh-shuh-**nahg**-ruh-furhz) scientists who study the oceans and seas and the living things in them

plains (**playnz**) large flat open areas of land that have no trees

pollution (puh-**loo**-shun) anything that dirties an environment, especially waste material

submarines (**suhb**-muh-reenz) boats that can work underwater

surface (**sehr**-fihs) the outside of anything

Resources

Books

What Is a Biome?
by Bobbie D. Kalman
Crabtree Publishing Company (1998)

The Dictionary of the Environment and Its Biomes
by Chris Myers (Editor)
Franklin Watts Incorporated (2001)

Web Sites

Due to the changing nature of Internet links, PowerKids Press has developed an on-line list of Web sites related to the subjects of this book. This site is updated regularly. Please use this link to access the list:

http://www.powerkidslinks.com/bio/ocn/

Index

C
currents, 12

E
energy, 6
erupt, 10
evaporate, 8–9

G
gravel, 6

M
mammals, 12–13
microscopes, 14
minerals, 6

O
oceanographers, 18

P
plains, 10
pollution, 20

S
submarines, 18
surface, 4, 10, 14

V
volcanoes, 10–11

Word Count: *475*

Note to Librarians, Teachers, and Parents

If reading is a challenge, Reading Power is a solution! Reading Power is perfect for readers who want high-interest subject matter at an accessible reading level. These fact-filled, photo-illustrated books are designed for readers who want straightforward vocabulary, engaging topics, and a manageable reading experience. With clear picture/text correspondence, leveled Reading Power books put the reader in charge. Now readers have the power to get the information they want and the skills they need in a user-friendly format.